Dr. Chevelta A. Smith. Email – info@drchevelta.com

Front Cover Book Design: Sanya Nicole, LLC
Editors: Ivory S. Bostick and Sandra Jones

Ordering Information:
Quantity sales. Special discounts are available on quantity purchases by corporations, associations, and others. For details, contact the "Special Sales Department" at the address above.

Can I Push? Journal Understanding the Process to Delivering Your Purpose/Dr. Chevelta A. Smith. —1st ed.
ISBN - 13: 978-0-9968295-1-9

Table of Contents

Introduction

I've always believed that anybody can be pregnant! No matter their gender, age, or ethnicity. Think about it! The word pregnant simply means to be "filled with." Medically speaking, this "filling" usually produces new life in the form of a baby. Personally speaking, I believe there are wonderful seeds of greatness (i.e.—talents, skills, passions, and dreams) placed in each of us at the beginning of our existence. When these seeds are fertilized with love, they will grow to "fill" us with new life and purpose. When this greatness is birthed, it too produces new life in ourselves and others around us. This is the manifestation of purpose.

So what are you pregnant with? An idea? A business? A book? A ministry? A college degree? Or an aspiration? Whatever it is, we all have greatness within that God intended for us to birth into the world. By birth, I simply mean that you are outwardly manifesting something that is inside of you for others to see and experience.

As you prepare to birth your amazing purpose, this **Can I Push? Journal** will give you an interactive approach to walk you thru this journey in the same way the journey to a natural birth occurs. This unique journal is designed to correspond to the 40'ish weeks of natural pregnancy. It helps you understand what you may be feeling, expecting, seeing, and experiencing during each stage of your journey.

In this Can I Push? Journal, you will find introspective questions, advice, and recommendations to help you manage the process to delivering the greatness in you. It is not only a companion to Dr. Smith's **Can I Push?** book, but also a one of a kind keepsake journal that is filled with reflections, discovery, and ways to track your personal growth—emotionally, spiritually, and physically.

So, What's inside of you awaiting to be birthed?

PRECONCEPTION

(Before the Pregnancy)

*P*reconception visits are extremely valuable for anyone desiring to birth new life. It is during this time that your OB/Gyn will assess your physical and emotional readiness to have a baby. How is your health? Are there any concerns regarding your ability to get pregnant? Do you have medical or social risks that may increase the likelihood of complications if you become pregnant? These are some of the many areas that will be evaluated. Stress, behavior, lifestyles, and certain attitudes can all be risks. The preconception appointment is a great time for your doctor to get to know you, and for you to get to know your body.

When starting the journey towards birthing your purpose, similar areas to birthing a child must be assessed. Although you won't need an OB/Gyn when preparing to deliver your purpose, you will need trustworthy individuals that can provide you with the same support and authentic relationships. More importantly, you too will have to commit not only to the journey, but to yourself. Be open with yourself. Be honest with yourself. Finally, unconditionally love yourself and embrace the changes you will make on this journey.

> "Knowing who you want to be in the future — requires that
> you first know who you are now."
>
> – C. A. Smith

About Me

Who are you, now?

_____

_____

_____   📷

_____   YOUR PHOTO HERE

_____

_____

_____

_____

_____

_____

_____

_____

_____

_____

_____

_____

_____

_____

Reflect on your answer above. **Is this who you want to be? Who do you desire to become? What does that person look like?** *Now, close your eyes and envision who you've always dreamed you would be.*

Who do you ultimately want to become?

_____

_____

_____

_____

_____

_____

_____

_____

_____

_____

Do you consider yourself a happy, sad, angry, fearful, shy, jealous, pessimistic, hopeful, guilt-filled, or apathetic person?
(Circle all that apply or you may add your own words below).

_____

_____

_____

_____

_____

_____

_____

_____

_____

What are your core values?

_____

_____

_____

_____

_____

_____

_____

_____

_____

_____

Things I need to change in my life physically, emotionally, spiritually, behaviorally, and relationally.

_____

_____

_____

_____

_____

_____

_____

_____

_____

_____

What is your dream job?

_____

_____

_____

_____

_____

_____

_____

_____

_____

_____

_____

_____

_____

_____

_____

_____

_____

_____

Support persons are very important, not only during pregnancy, but also at the time of birth. This will also hold true as you prepare to deliver the greatness and purpose that is developing inside of you.

Make an appointment to meet (via phone or face-to-face) with trusting individuals that you believe will genuinely support you throughout this journey. Share with each that you are beginning a journey to learn how to birth the greatness that is in you. You may also share some of your above answers with them. Ask them to be your support and explain why you chose them.

Date: /   /   M T W T F S S   Time:

From the very moment little girls are born, millions of immature eggs are present within their ovaries. Each egg is a woman's seed that waits for the moment it will be released to create new life.

From birth until puberty, many of the eggs will die, leaving her only a few hundred thousand eggs available to reproduce.

Ideas, dreams, and goals are often seeds that lie within each of us.

What ideas and/or personal goals are presently inside of you, awaiting their release?

_____

_____

_____

_____

_____

_____

_____

_____

_____

_____

_____

_____

_____

_____

_____

_____

_____

_____

_____

_____

_____

_____

How will these dreams and goals create new life in you or others?

_____

_____

_____

_____

_____

_____

_____

_____

_____

_____

_____

_____

_____

_____

_____

_____

_____

_____

_____

_____

_____

_____

_____

_____

_____

_____

_____

_____

Can you think of specific dreams you once had, but allowed to die?
If so, why did you give up on them?

Which of the above dreams/goals do you still desire to pursue?

_____

_____

_____

_____

_____

_____

_____

_____

_____

_____

_____

_____

_____

_____

_____

_____

_____

_____

_____

_____

_____

_____

_____

_____

_____

_____

_____

_____

_____

_____

Create an action plan below to achieve your desired life goals.

1.

2.

3.

4.

5.

6.

7.

8.

9.

10.

🖊 **Note to self:** *Discuss this action plan with my support people to help keep me accountable.*

_____

_____

_____

_____

_____

$\mathcal{S}$tress, worry, and negative thoughts can adversely impact pregnancy. It's also been said that the developing fetus can feel what his or her expectant mommy feels—good or bad—while in the womb.

Positive thinking is important throughout the entire pregnancy process. It is a powerful weapon against fear, anxiety, and "stinking thinking" that have the potential to jeopardize a healthy pregnancy outcome.

Like normal human pregnancy—stress, anxiety, fear, negative thoughts and attitudes can jeopardize the healthy pregnancy outcome of delivering your purpose and the greatness inside of you.

Write a personal affirmation that you can refer to throughout this journey to delivering your purpose.

I've provided an example below:

I have greatness in me.

I have great ideas and great purpose.

I have everything inside of me to be successful.

I have everything inside of me to live happy.

I am strong.

I am healthy.

I am intelligent.

I have the capacity to produce love, forgiveness, and peace.

I am no longer broken.

I am healed.

I will not abort the purpose that God has placed in me.

I will grow and develop into the positive person I was meant to be.

I am complete.

Pregnancy Affirmation:

Pregnancy Affirmation:

In obstetrics, a woman's ability to conceive is less dependent upon the number of seeds that lie within her ovaries. It is the quality of the ovulated (released) egg that is key. Only mature eggs can manifest new life. Mature, meaning fully developed.

In comparison, when desiring to deliver purpose—faith must be released. This faith, however, must be mature just like the egg released from a woman's ovary. More importantly, this fully developed faith should be the seed covering for the ideas, dreams, and goals that will produce the greatness inside of you. Without faith being released in the seeds of your greatness—your purpose will not be manifested. Faith is key.

Do you believe that you can and will manifest the purpose and greatness within you?

_____

_____

_____

_____

_____

_____

_____

_____

_____

_____

If God were to examine your faith, would He find it "too little" or "more than enough?" Explain.

_____

_____

_____

_____

_____

_____

_____

_____

_____

_____

_____

_____

_____

_____

_____

_____

_____

_____

_____

_____

_____

_____

_____

_____

_____

_____

_____

_____

_____

_____

_____

_____

_____

_____

_____

How do you rate your faith in yourself?

☐ Excellent   ☐ Good   ☐ Average   ☐ Poor   ☐ Non-existent

What steps can you take to fully develop and improve the quality of your faith?

_____

_____

_____

_____

_____

_____

_____

_____

_____

_____

_____

_____

_____

_____

_____

_____

_____

_____

_____

_____

_____

_____

_____

_____

Note to self: Consider finding and/or joining a church or support group to help grow your faith.

The physiological process leading to the release of a mature egg from the ovary is very complex. The ability for the egg to be released from the ovary does not rely on the ovary alone. In fact, if a certain area in the brain does not release the hormone needed to directly stimulate the ovary, then release of the egg will not occur. If there is no release of an egg—then pregnancy cannot occur.

Likewise, faith works to transform our mindset in a way that stimulates the release of the seeds of our purpose.

What specific mindsets do you have that are hindering your ability to release the wonderful gifts and talents you possess?

Take a moment to recite your Personal Affirmation aloud.

How do you feel after reciting your affirmation?

☐ Empowered   ☐ More confident   ☐ Energized   ☐ Other: _____

_____
_____
_____
_____
_____
_____
_____
_____
_____
_____
_____
_____
_____
_____
_____
_____
_____
_____

🖊 **Note to self:** Continue reciting positive affirmations to myself. They allow my mind to transform its negative thoughts into positive attitudes.

"When we have faith, it allows God room to come into our lives and make what we thought was impossible — possible."

–C. A. Smith

*P*eople do not get pregnant by themselves. A sexual or medical encounter must take place. The ability to reproduce is not a solo act. Who my patients are partnered with can impact the pregnancy process in so many ways. Therefore, as an Obstetrician, it is important for me to know if she is connected with someone who will love and support her, as well as, the gift she will birth in the future.

Name the individuals you are connected to and who consistently
demonstrates a desire to see you reach your fullest potential.

_____

_____

_____

_____

_____

_____

_____

_____

_____

_____

_____

_____

_____

_____

Do you have any sexual or emotional ties that present a risk of
compromising the greatness in you?

_____

_____

_____

_____

_____

_____

_____

Create an action plan to safely disconnect from those relationships which are harmful or negatively impacting you. Discuss with trusted support persons.

1.

2.

3.

4.

5.

6.

7.

8.

9.

10.

Note to self: It's okay for me to seek professional counseling to disconnect from relationships that are harmful to me emotionally, spiritually, and physically.

> "Who you become sexually involved with is who you become connected to spiritually and emotionally."
>
> — C.A. Smith

In obstetrics, regular ovulation and intercourse alone are not enough for pregnancy to take place. There is much more to this process that leads to pregnancy. Once the egg is released from the ovary, it must be fertilized by the seed of a male partner (sperm) in order for pregnancy to even have a chance to develop. Fertilization and conception requires a deposit.

Do you allow other people to deposit seeds of negativity into your heart and mind? If so, why?

When you are regularly releasing faith and connecting to those who have your best interest at heart, you become ready for God's love to be deposited in your heart. It's this love that fertilizes the seeds of greatness within you. Once fertilized, these seeds begin to grow and manifest new life.

What changes do you feel taking place in you since beginning this journey to delivering your purpose?

_____

_____

_____

_____

_____

_____

_____

_____

_____

_____

_____

_____

_____

_____

_____

_____

_____

_____

_____

_____

_____

_____

Have you considered a relationship with God in order to discover every seed of greatness and purpose that He deposited in you when He created you?

_____

_____

_____

_____

_____

_____

_____

_____

_____

In an effort to prevent pregnancy, contraception is used by many. Similarly, many of us make it very difficult for God to enter our lives and create new life.

Have you put up barriers to keep others out, including God?

_____

_____

_____

_____

_____

_____

_____

_____

_____

_____

_____

onfirmation of pregnancy is essential in Obstetrics. Sadly, the home pregnancy test is not always accurate. As a result, it can sometimes yield a false negative or positive result.

The same thing can happen in life. We feel and know that something great is developing inside of us; yet when we seek the confirmation of others, we can often be given the wrong result. This is why you cannot always rely on the ability of others to detect the gifts that God has placed in you.

Take a moment to reflect. **Do you rely solely on the ability of others to identify the wonderful gifts and talents that God has placed inside of you? If so, why?**

_____

_____

_____

_____

_____

_____

_____

_____

_____

_____

_____

_____

_____

_____

_____

_____

_____

_____

_____

_____

_____

_____

_____

_____

_____

_____

In response to your answer above, **write an apology letter to yourself.** Ask for forgiveness for lacking confidence and belief in yourself. **Release** past hurts, disappointments, and mistakes that you've allowed to keep you in the bondage of shame, regret or self-hate. **Seek** to start over in a loving relationship with yourself. **Commit** to learning who the person (your name) is now. If deep wounds and scars exist, **promise yourself** that you will take all necessary steps to ensure your healing, even if it means seeking medical attention.

_____

_____

_____

_____

_____

_____

_____

_____

_____

_____

_____

_____

_____

_____

_____

_____

_____

_____

_____

_____

_____

_____

Note to self: *I will never again, doubt the seeds of great ideas, talents, skills, creativity, etc. that God has placed inside of me. I will trust God's loving words about me, over the words of others.*

FIRST TRIMESTER
(Weeks 1-12)

When a woman discovers she is pregnant, many different feelings may arise. As an OB/Gyn, fear, excitement, nervousness, and joy are a few of the emotions I've witnessed in many of my patients.

When did you realize that you were "filled with" (pregnant) with greatness?

_____

_____

_____

_____

_____

_____

Do you remember the specific date that you were able to positively identify your greatness?

_____

_____

_____

_____

_____

_____

How did you feel in that moment?

_____

_____

_____

_____

_____

_____

Soon after learning that they are pregnant, many women begin to worry about losing the baby. In fact, a great deal of women are so overwhelmed with the thought of pregnancy failure that they often won't announce to others that they are pregnant until after the first trimester. Sadly, their reason is because they do not want to experience the embarrassment of failing to carry their new pregnancy to term.

Do you have a fear of failure regarding your ability to be successful academically, professionally, spiritually, etc.?

_____

_____

_____

_____

_____

_____

In what areas of your life are you afraid that you will fail?

_____

_____

_____

_____

_____

_____

When and where do you believe this fear of failure originated for you?

_____

_____

_____

_____

_____

_____

_____

_____

_____

**What can you do to overcome the fear of failure in the areas of your life
listed above?**

Write the plan below. Discuss with your support persons.

_____

_____

_____

_____

_____

_____

_____

_____

_____

_____

_____

_____

_____

_____

_____

_____

_____

_____

_____

_____

_____

_____

Write the name(s) of your support person(s) and tell how he/she specifically supports you.

_____

_____

_____

_____

_____

_____

_____

PHOTO OF SUPPORT PERSON(S) HERE

*P*regnancy requires sacrifice. A Mom-to-Be is often instructed to give up various foods, behavior, and activities that can compromise the health and wellness of the new life that will develop inside of her. Alcohol, smoking, high fall risk activities are amongst the things she is encouraged to avoid. Additionally, countless women develop an intolerance for certain foods and smells which often leads to nausea and/or vomiting. For many, this is usually a common sign of pregnancy.

What behavior, activities, or individuals have you noticed that you have given up since discovering the purpose that lies in you?

_____

_____

_____

_____

_____

_____

_____

_____

_____

_____

_____

_____

_____

What other things or individuals do you need to disconnect from to ensure that the health and well-being of the greatness in you are not compromised or aborted?

_____

_____

_____

_____

_____

_____

_____

In the first trimester, although many changes are occurring within the body of my patients—I cannot see it. In fact, no one can. Nevertheless, there is no doubt she is carrying new life within her. We have a knowing due to our confirmation testing. She has a feeling due to the symptoms she is experiencing. Finally, there is a hearing. The evidence of new life developing within, as the sound of that little heart beating, is heard with a special device.

Same process takes place when we become pregnant (filled) with our purpose. We know there is a newness within us and want so badly for others to see it. Unfortunately, they can't. It's not time.

In the first trimester of your pregnancy with purpose, the greatness in you has been fertilized to grow. New inspiration and motivation often occur during this period. General ideas now become more detailed concepts. This season of development is specifically focused on internal transformation and change. Be patient. Feel what God is doing and hear what He, and those that He has placed in your life, are saying. In time, there will be a manifestation of the greatness that is developing in you.

How are you feeling today?

_____
_____
_____
_____
_____
_____
_____
_____
_____
_____
_____
_____
_____
_____
_____

How do you currently view yourself compared to when you were at the beginning of this journey?

_____
_____
_____
_____
_____
_____
_____
_____

What new changes have you noticed in your attitude or thinking?

_____

_____

_____

_____

_____

_____

_____

_____

_____

_____

_____

_____

_____

What things have you heard or are currently listening to for inspiration and motivation?

_____

_____

_____

_____

_____

_____

_____

Are you struggling with impatience? How?

> *"Stand firm, and you will win life"*
> *– Luke 21:19 (NIV).*

Take a moment to ask God to give you patience. Affirm yourself by reciting the quote at the top of this page. Rewrite it below as the following action plan: *"I will stand firm (patiently), and I will win life."* Repeat it daily.

_____

_____

_____

_____

_____

_____

_____

Find other affirmations, quotes, or scriptures to help increase your patience.

_____

_____

_____

_____

_____

_____

_____

_____

_____

_____

_____

"*I wait for the Lord, my whole being waits, and in His word I put my hope.*"

– Psalm 130:5 (NIV)

In the first few weeks of the first trimester, the fetal cells have been dividing and multiplying. Initially, the cells were a ball of cells that all looked and functioned the same. They are identical in composition and express no difference. Throughout this trimester, the purpose of each cell begins to unfold. Eventually, each cell begins to migrate to the part of the body in which it was created to function (brain, leg, stomach, heart, etc.)

During this time in your pregnancy with purpose, you may begin to feel more aware of what your specific function and purpose in life may be. This unfolding, regarding the depths of your gifts, is often revealed by God Himself as you spend time in reflection and meditation. You become different and begin to feel a "pulling" into certain areas academically, professionally, spiritually, etc. You begin to feel a true "sense of purpose." This is evidence that you are growing.

> "When God penetrates your heart, you become different."
> – C. A. Smith

In what ways are you beginning to feel a "true sense" of purpose?

_____

_____

_____

_____

_____

_____

_____

In what ways do you believe you are becoming different?

_____

_____

_____

_____

_____

_____

_____

_____

_____

_____

_____

_____

_____

In what specific area of your life do you feel a "pulling or tugging" in your heart to do something?

_____

_____

_____

_____

_____

_____

_____

_____

_____

_____

_____

_____

_____

_____

_____

_____

_____

_____

_____

_____

_____

_____

_____

_____

_____

By this time, as well, you may have started to notice your appetite for certain things has changed. "Cravings" begin to manifest and you find yourself liking things that you never imagined you would.

What things are you craving to do? Are they positive or negative?

_____

_____

_____

_____

_____

_____

_____

_____

_____

_____

_____

_____

_____

_____

_____

_____

_____

_____

✐ **Note to self:** *I must make sure that what I crave to do will not negatively impact the great purpose that is developing in me. I commit to staying accountable to my support team/person to ensure that the changes I am making are appropriate for healthy growth.*

SECOND TRIMESTER
(Weeks 13-27)

The second trimester is all about internal growth that now becomes visibly manifested. During these weeks, the "belly bump" that every pregnant woman is anticipating—becomes evident. Everyone can now see that there is something growing inside of her. That something is new life.

Although every cell needed to develop each specific part of the human body is present at the beginning of this trimester, each cell must still transform into its specified body part. Heart cells develop into the heart. Lung cells develop into the lungs, etc. Growth and development are what this trimester is all about. Belly measurements by the OB/Gyn are key during this time to assess appropriate growth. Growth is important because we know that things are maturing when they grow.

Spiritually, physically, emotionally—your growth should begin "to show" during this time in your pregnancy with purpose. Making regular times to talk or meet with your support person(s) is critical. This allows routine "checks" for adequate growth.

In what areas have you noticed obvious growth in yourself?

_____

_____

_____

_____

_____

_____

_____

_____

_____

_____

_____

_____

_____

_____

_____

_____

_____

_____

_____

_____

_____

_____

_____

_____

_____

_____

Belly checks involve measuring the size of the uterus. The measurement in centimeters should correspond closely to the number of weeks a woman has been pregnant.

Do you feel that you have been growing adequately thus far in your journey?

_____

_____

_____

_____

_____

_____

_____

_____

_____

_____

_____

_____

_____

_____

_____

_____

_____

_____

_____

_____

_____

_____

"God has placed everything in you that is needed to be victorious in your life."

– C. A. Smith

How do you feel about the growth you've been seeing in yourself?

_____

_____

_____

_____

_____

_____

_____

_____

_____

_____

_____

_____

_____

_____

_____

_____

_____

_____

_____

_____

_____

_____

_____

What have others expressed regarding the growth they are seeing?

_____

_____

_____

_____

_____

_____

_____

_____

_____

_____

_____

YOUR PHOTO HERE

Do you have that pregnancy glow?

What is different about yourself in this picture compared to the previous one?

_____

_____

_____

_____

_____

_____

_____

_____

_____

_____

_____

Do you see a noticeable change in your

☐ demeanor   ☐ grooming   ☐ physical appearance   ☐ Other _____

_____

_____

_____

_____

_____

_____

_____

_____

_____

_____

_____

$\mathcal{B}$etween 18-20 weeks is the most awaited time frame within every pregnancy. Why? Because—this is when the expectant mother finds out the answer to the number one question she's frequently asked. "What are you having—a boy or a girl?"

Up until now, many women have chosen to hold off from painting the nursery, purchasing baby items, or determining names. Although preparing for the birth of her baby, she has intentionally placed limitations on how much detailed preparation she would execute. Mostly, because she desires to be intentional in her planning.

Her preparation is primarily focused internally. Reading pregnancy books, talking with others who have already experienced birth, and asking lots of questions of her OB/Gyn are ways she readies herself.

What are you having?
(i.e. – a book, business, ministry, degree, career, or other?)

_____

_____

_____

_____

_____

_____

_____

_____

_____

How will you intentionally prepare for the delivery of this greatness?

_____

_____

_____

_____

_____

_____

_____

_____

_____

_____

_____

_____

_____

Although there are some exciting things that occur in the second trimester (i.e. – visibility of the baby bump and feeling the baby kick for the first time), there are also some not so exciting things that develop during these weeks leading up to the third trimester.

Towards the mid to later part of the second trimester, my patients begin to experience what I call the "normal aches and quakes of pregnancy." Pressure and pain begin to emerge. The excitement for some, starts to fade. They begin to focus on the discomfort experienced vs. the necessary process. Complaining arises for some. Others may become fatigued. The discomfort, for many, causes them to move slower or barely at all. This is the time that encouragement and support are essential. Likewise, exercise and continued mobility is advised.

When getting closer to delivering the greatness within you, the experience is often the same. This is the time when many lose momentum. Self-encouragement and affirmation are vital during this specific period of growth. They are weapons against complaining and self-sabotage.

What pressure are you feeling presently?

_____

_____

_____

_____

_____

_____

_____

_____

_____

_____

_____

_____

_____

How are you coping?

_____

_____

_____

_____

_____

_____

_____

_____

_____

_____

_____

_____

_____

_____

_____

_____

_____

_____

_____

_____

_____

_____

_____

_____

Write down specific times each day of the week that you will commit to personal stress relief activities. List the planned activity.

Sunday	
Monday	
Tuesday	
Wednesday	
Thursday	
Friday	
Saturday	

Physical exercise is encouraged throughout pregnancy. Contrary to patient beliefs, it does not increase the risk for miscarriage or preterm labor/ delivery. Back pain relief, increased energy, improved mood, and improved labor outcomes are a few fitness benefits.

Are you exercising on a regular basis? If no, why not?

_____

_____

_____

_____

_____

_____

_____

_____

_____

_____

_____

_____

_____

_____

_____

_____

_____

_____

Make an appointment with your doctor to discuss an exercise plan.

Date: /   /   M T W T F S S   Time:

Name of doctor:

THIRD TRIMESTER

(Weeks 28-40'ish)

$\mathcal{T}$hroughout the third trimester, my patient's belly is becoming larger and larger. Towards the end of this trimester, rapid growth of the fetus is taking place as the Mom-to-Be nears her expected date of delivery. Uterine measurements and fetal heart tones continue to be monitored. Although the focus still remains on growth, the third trimester is all about maturity. Maturation of the developing fetus and preparation for delivery is important during these final weeks.

Increased discomfort from the enlarging baby and uterus continue. Frustration is at an all-time high. Lack of rest increases due to my patient's inability to find comfortable positions during sleep. She is tired, especially mentally. The weight of what is growing inside of her intensifies. She becomes tired of the process and desires it to end. She often expresses, "I just want the baby out!"

This same feeling arises in many as they near the appointed time to deliver their purpose.

In what ways are you continuing to grow?

As you progress further in this pregnancy with purpose, are you noticing an enlargement in your ability to (circle): love, forgive, express joy, have peace, demonstrate self-control, and release faith? Explain.

_____

_____

_____

_____

_____

_____

_____

_____

_____

_____

_____

_____

_____

_____

_____

_____

_____

_____

_____

_____

_____

_____

_____

_____

_____

What are you doing to ensure you are getting rest—physically, emotionally, and spiritually?

_____

_____

_____

_____

_____

_____

_____

_____

_____

_____

_____

_____

_____

_____

_____

_____

_____

_____

_____

_____

_____

In the last part of the third trimester, appointments with the OB/Gyn are weekly vs. the initial monthly.

🖉 **Note to self:** *Make time to connect with my support person(s) more frequently during this season of my life.*

At 37 weeks of pregnancy, the expectant mother is considered "term." To become term is the ultimate goal of every pregnancy. This simply means to become mature. Any pregnancy that occurs before 37 weeks by definition is preterm. Preterm labor can cause major complications to the health and life of the baby.

Maturation is the process of obtaining full development and growth.
A fetus is considered to be mature if it had a specific amount of time in the uterus and placental support to make growth possible. You cannot have one without the other.

In the same way, these are critical factors in the maturation of one's purpose and greatness that have been developing. Support systems provide protection, accountability, safety, and fellowship. Having a specific time in this type of growing environment should lead to the maturation of the greatness inside of you.

Date: / /

> "Maturity requires time and support."
>
> – C.A.Smith

In what ways have you matured while on this journey?

_____

_____

_____

_____

_____

_____

_____

_____

_____

_____

_____

_____

_____

_____

_____

_____

_____

_____

_____

_____

_____

_____

YOUR PHOTO HERE

Do you feel you need more time to reach maturation in other areas?

_____

_____

_____

_____

_____

_____

_____

_____

_____

_____

_____

_____

_____

_____

_____

Have you maintained a well-established support system throughout this pregnancy with purpose?

_____

_____

_____

_____

_____

_____

_____

_____

_____

_____

If no, how will you work to re-establish the necessary support system?

_____

_____

_____

_____

_____

_____

_____

_____

_____

_____

Create an action plan to re-establish your support system.

1.

2.

3.

4.

5.

6.

7.

8.

9.

10.

✏️ **Note to self:** *I will continue to prepare, grow, and mature until the time to deliver the greatness in me arrives. Until that time, I will be patient. I trust that God will let me know when it will be time to push out my purpose.*

LABOR & DELIVERY

$\mathcal{U}$p until the time of labor, the uterus has been in a quiescent state. It has simply served as a safe harbor for the new life that has been growing inside of it. Throughout pregnancy, the size of the uterus has been getting bigger and bigger. Finally, it reaches maximum stretch. Its capacity is completely filled with new life. There is no more room to grow. The baby must be birthed into the larger space of the world, where he or she will continue to grow outwardly.

At an appointed time, unbeknownst to any man, uterine stimulating hormones begin to awaken the suppressed uterus. The awakening of the uterus triggers an electrical impulse throughout its muscles. The result— the infamous painful contraction. With each contraction, an intensifying force is generated to move the baby down the birth canal. Soon, this gift of life will be expulsed.

In what areas of your life are you currently feeling stretched?

_____

_____

_____

_____

_____

_____

_____

_____

_____

How are you handling the physical and emotional stress during this time?

_____

_____

_____

_____

_____

_____

_____

_____

✎ **Note to self:** Make a time to connect with my support person(s) if feeling overwhelmed.

Date: /   /   M T W T F S S   Time: ....

As an Obstetrician, I am concerned with how well my patient is progressing in labor. Although pregnancy is about process, labor and delivery is all about progress. In other words, it's about forward movement and advancement. Specifically—change.

Even though many things are changing during the labor phase, the main focus is cervical change. The cervix is the doorway to the birth canal. At the beginning of pregnancy, it is closed tightly, however, in normal labor, the force of contractions causes it to soften and open. Once opened completely, birth can take place.

Progress is determined by how well the cervix is opening. It should make a certain amount of change within a specific time frame. Physical exams of the cervix must be performed to verify if adequate change is occurring. Slow or no progression can usually be a sign that something is wrong and warrants further investigation.

> *"Examinations are mandatory in determining progression."*
>
> – C.A.Smith

Take a moment to examine your heart, as you near the time to push out your purpose. **Has it opened and softened more throughout this journey?**

_____

_____

_____

_____

_____

_____

_____

_____

How has your heart changed?

_____

_____

_____

_____

_____

_____

_____

_____

_____

_____

What areas of your heart remain hardened (firm) and unchanged?

_____

_____

_____

_____

_____

_____

_____

_____

_____

_____

When God is softening and dilating your heart, like contractions, this can be a very painful process because often times it requires you to face painful realities about yourself and others.

Take a closer look within your heart. **Did you discover unforgiveness, hatred, or resentment? If so, from where does it stem?**

_____

_____

_____

_____

_____

_____

_____

_____

_____

Create an action plan to heal the hardened areas in your heart that are prohibiting your ability to progress forward in delivering your purpose.

1.

2.

3.

4.

5.

6.

7.

8.

9.

10.

*L*abor pain creates the pressure necessary to deliver what lies inside the expectant mother. It is purposed to push out the new baby that has finally matured. When the cervix becomes fully dilated (100%), then the time to push has finally arrived.

Pushing is hard work. Many of my patients must learn to relax their bodies and stop fighting against the contraction. Pushing requires not only instruction, coaching, and support—but more importantly—permission. My patients understand the need to wait for my consent to push. Pushing outside of the appropriate timing, can cause harm to both mom and fetus.

When delivering purpose, it is just as important that you wait until you receive instruction to push. During this stage, it's important that you relax and quiet yourself enough to hear God's still small voice. Trust me, He will speak. His instructions are important because they will help facilitate this stage of labor. If you can remain focused on His directives, you will ultimately birth the purpose you've been anticipating.

Are you starting to feel an urge to push out the greatness within?

_____

_____

_____

What exactly have you been feeling?
(i.e.- frustration, worry, excitement, stress, or tiredness?)

_____

_____

_____

_____

_____

_____

_____

_____

Are you spending daily time in prayer to receive instruction from God?
If not, why?

_____

_____

_____

_____

_____

_____

_____

_____

Write the instructions or counsel you've received from your support person(s), God, or others during this time of pushing out your purpose.

1.

2.

3.

4.

5.

6.

7.

8.

9.

10.

How are you keeping your focus while pushing out your purpose?

_____

_____

_____

_____

_____

_____

_____

_____

_____

_____

_____

_____

_____

_____

_____

_____

_____

_____

_____

_____

_____

🖊 **Note to self:** Pushing out my greatness, like human birth, can sometimes take much longer than I anticipated. More importantly—I must remember, that my timing to deliver will often be different from others. I must not compare my journey to the journey of others. I must not get discouraged. I will remain focused, until the fullness of my delivery has come.

When a baby is being born, its reveal occurs in different phases. The head is delivered first, followed by the shoulders, and finally the body.

Are you starting to see glimpses of your greatness being manifested?
(i.e. – business, specific goals or dreams, etc.)

_____

_____

_____

_____

_____

_____

_____

_____

What specific part(s) of your purpose is visible?

_____

_____

_____

_____

_____

_____

_____

_____

_____

_____

_____

When did you finally deliver the fullness of your purpose?

Date: /   /   M T W T F S S   Time:

How do you feel?

_____

_____

_____

_____

_____

> *"To everything there is a season,*
> *A time for every purpose under heaven*
> *A time to be born. . ." (Ecclesiates 3:1-2, NKJV)*

PHOTO OF YOUR MANIFESTED GREATNESS/PURPOSE
HERE
(business, book, degree, etc.)

Congratulations **on your birth!** *You* **did it!**

www.ingramcontent.com/pod-product-compliance
Lightning Source LLC
Chambersburg PA
CBHW041821090426

42811CB00009B/1067